The Twelve Days of Christmas

COWLEY PUBLICATIONS is a ministry of the brothers of the Society of Saint John the Evangelist, a monastic order in the Episcopal Church. Our mission is to provide books and resources for those seeking spiritual and theological formation. COWLEY PUBLICATIONS is committed to developing a new generation of writers and teachers who will encourage people to think and pray in new ways about spirituality, reconciliation, and the future.

The Twelve Days of Christmas

Unwrapping the Gifts

Curtis G. Almquist, SSJE

Cowley Publications

CAMBRIDGE, MASSACHUSETTS

Published in the United States of America by Cowley Publications, a division of the Society of Saint John the Evangelist. No portion of this book may be reproduced, stored in or introduced into a retrieval system, or transmitted, in any form or by any means—including photocopying—without the prior written permission of Cowley Publications, except in the case of brief quotations embedded in critical articles and reviews.

Library of Congress
Cataloging-in-Publication Data

Almquist, Curtis G., 1952-
   The twelve days of Christmas : unwrapping the gifts / Curtis G. Almquist.
      p.   cm.
   Includes bibliographical references.
   ISBN-10: 1-56101-293-9
   ISBN-13: 978-1-56101-293-0
   (pbk. : alk. paper)
   1. Christmas—Meditations.
   I. Title.
   BV45.A58   2006
   242'.335—dc22

               2006014490

Scripture quotations are taken from The New Revised Standard Version of the Bible, © 1989, by the Division of Christian Education of the National Council of the Churches of Christ in the United States of America. Used by permission.

Cover design: Kyle G. Hunter
Interior design: Wendy Holdman

This book was printed in Canada on acid-free paper.

Cowley Publications
4 Brattle Street
Cambridge, Massachusetts 02138
800-225-1534 • www.cowley.org

To my parents, for their gift of life.

Contents

Introduction

*C*HRISTMAS, ANTICIPATED so many months ahead, taps a great need of the soul to give and receive gifts. If you look at the glossy magazine that comes with the Sunday newspaper, read the signs on storefronts and billboards, see the ads on television or the internet, you find many promises. Some of these promises are quite subliminal, and yet they clearly tap a need. The need is not necessarily for the particular gift being advertised, but rather for the experience we will realize if we give or receive this gift. Whether it is clothing or perfume, a beverage or a pastry, a jewel or even a telephone calling card, we are promised to receive something more. So what is it that's really being marketed? Particular gifts promise to satisfy our need to belong, our need for self-esteem and recognition, our need to be attractive and desired, our need to appear successful and valuable, our thirst for the real thing, our desire to stay young and even childlike, and our longing for immortality.

Those whose business is marketing these gifts understand that we are all looking for something more. And this much is true: the soul does crave something more because we have been created in the image of God, who is more. If we don't satisfy our infinite longing for what is more, we do settle for something that is less—and through repeated doses of various lesser goods, we try relentlessly and inadequately to quench our infinite cravings at Christmas and throughout our lifetimes.

The twelve days of Christmas run from December 26 through January 6, the Feast of the Epiphany, the date on which we traditionally recall the Magi's arrival to present gifts to the infant Jesus. For many, the sacred meaning of these days is lost. By Christmas night we are already saturated with the holiday hype, overfed with music and food, and maybe quite disappointed that the presents we received have not fulfilled us.

The reflections that follow are not a "bah humbug" about Christmas customs and presents. They are simply an invitation to go deeper than the tinsel and wrappings to the source of all the good gifts in life. As you pray over the course of the twelve days of Christmas, I invite you to unwrap gifts that will last and that will satisfy your spiritual cravings.

The Twelve Days of Christmas

DECEMBER 26

The Gift of Love

GOD LOVES YOU. Who you are, what you are, how you've gotten to be where you are: God knows and loves all that. God has this passionate love affair going on with you. God has created you as you are, cherishes you, and longs for your companionship. God has plans for a relationship with you that lasts forever and that grows in intimacy over time. It's like an eternal infatuation. When you're sleeping, God is dreaming up ways to be with you. When you're working or walking or weeping, God is catching up with you in the wind across your face, in the singing of a bird, in the free fall of laughter, in the soothing touch of a friend. You are the apple of God's eye.

We find our life energies drawing on this love of God for us. We have been created to be "rooted and grounded in love" (Ephesians 3:17). A plant or tree draws its stability and nourishment from the root system in order to grow and soar into the light. But it's quite possible to be grounded in a way that is not life-giving. We run the risk of running aground, like a ship at sea can become grounded in shallow water, stuck, perhaps at risk of sinking.

One way of running aground is to get stuck in resentment, envy, or jealousy. Perhaps there's something about our own life where we find ourselves coming up short compared to someone else's life, which we eye. Perhaps we haven't been recognized as they have, or maybe that recognition has been negative. Perhaps we've been given certain work to do or not been given certain work to do. Maybe the way in which we have been negatively recognized has something to do with our education, our family of origin, our physical appearance, our charm, our eloquence, our finances. Whatever might be the case, we find ourselves not as favored as someone else whom we think we could have been or should have been. So we find ourselves run aground, stuck in a kind of comparative resentment. This is certainly not the same as being "rooted and grounded in love."

We are set free from these shallow waters and rocks by saying *yes* to our own lives, *yes* to the life God has given us.

I think many of us have at some point awakened to realize that the role we've been handed in the play of life is not the part we were trying out for. Say yes to your life, but do not say it as a passive victim, letting one bad thing after another roll over you and finding a kind of perverse enjoyment in being miserable. For when Jesus says that he's come "to give us life, and to give it to us abundantly" (John 10:10), he means life is to be seized with eager anticipation, like a child eagerly reaching out to a present being offered. So receive life as a gift, not simply as a given. Cherish your life. Savor it, every moment of every day. Don't miss a minute of the life that God is offering you.

An old monastic insight is that freedom is to be found in the context of limitations. You cannot have it all. The sky is *not* the limit. There are certain constraints. Saying yes to life, accepting the things that cannot be changed, means coming to terms with everything life could have been or, we may feel, should have been, but isn't. The real presence of God is really found in the present time, given all its opportunities and limitations.

What then is this life for which we have been created? We have been created in the love of God and for the love of God. Love is the essence of who we are. When we find ourselves outside of love, it's a sign that there's a constriction somewhere in our root system. This constriction is repairable because love is the essence of who we have been created to be, in the image of God, who is love. We have been created to be rooted and grounded in life-giving love.

We can tell whether we are living in the love of God by asking ourselves what we worship. Worship is about ascribing ultimate worth and meaning to something. Will your worship last a lifetime and see you into eternity? Or will it have to go? If your theology is predicated on forever having good health and a sense of certainty that you will never know diminishment, you are giving ultimate meaning to something that won't last. If your theology is predicated on your job security or career advancement, on your being held in high esteem, on your being in control, then your theology isn't big enough. If your theology is predicated on certain political configurations, on the unchanging structure of the Church, or on financial independence, then it's nothing to bank on. God is the beginning and end of life. Life is on God's terms, and God is very jealous. God shares life with us as gift, *gratis*, from which comes our word *grace*. Life is a gift. If your theology is no bigger than your mortality, it's too small and won't last.

Someone has said that the Gospel—the good news—is bad news before it is good news. The bad news is that our lives are incomplete, perhaps even unmanageable, without the God who created us. If you've run aground, you may need to be rescued, saved. The good news is that God knows it. That God knows you and loves you makes it not just good news but terrific news! For God is offering you the gift of love.

The Gift of Revelation

F I WERE TO DESCRIBE someone as "a real dreamer," you would probably have a rather dubious impression of that person. If I were to tell about a plan that "someone had just dreamed up," it would probably sound like a scheme or something quite naïve, and probably not like a plan in which you would put much stock. We are prone to bank on what has empirical validity: what we can quantify or dissect or anchor in concrete reality. But my hunch is that for many of us, a deeper way of knowing, a subconscious channel of meaning or leading, flows into our soul. This is certainly true of the Christmas story recorded in the Gospels, which is chock-full of dreams and revelations. Here are some snapshots drawn from the nativity story as told in the Gospel of Matthew.

Mary discovers she is pregnant, not by Joseph and not by another man, but by the Holy Spirit. This would seem a bit of a stretch. We know that Mary's story is simply to repeat what had been said to her. By whom? An angel. Let's say if a young woman came to you and told you a similar story about being touched by an angel, it would probably give you pause. But Joseph, we hear, is a just and honorable man. Though the Law gives him every reason to publicly denounce Mary's rather obvious and disgraceful "fornication," if for no other reason than to save his own good name, he elects to "dismiss Mary quietly." There's something quite beautiful here about his respecting her dignity, even with this concocted story she is telling. And then something happens. Joseph dreams. In his dream he is told *not* to be afraid and *not* to leave Mary. He is told that this is a good and blessed thing of God that actually *has* happened to Mary, and that they indeed should be married. That revelation came in a dream, and Joseph staked his life (and Mary's life and Jesus' life) on a dream.

The next snapshot concerns the wise men, the astrologers who live "in the east." Something compels them to be looking for this long-predicted Messiah. How do they end up finding this Christ child, this Messiah? They follow a star.

Do *you* follow stars? What if someone asked you why you bought a particular piece of real estate, and you answered, "I followed a star"? Yikes. People would probably begin politely stepping away from you. What about the wise men? They follow a star to the Christ child and bring their gifts of gold, frankincense, and myrrh. On leaving they are warned to return home by another way because King Herod is on the prowl. How are they warned? A dream, which they believe and follow. A star. Then a dream.

The third snapshot: Once these wise men leave, Joseph is given a similar warning about King Herod, who is searching for this child to destroy him. Joseph is told to flee to Egypt for safety: "Go now!" And Joseph takes Mary and Jesus and they flee. How is Joseph warned? A dream, which he believes. The fourth snapshot: The threatening King Herod dies. Joseph learns about it, and is told that it is now safe to return to the land of Israel, which he does. How is he told this? Through a dream, which he believes. The fifth snapshot: Joseph and the family no sooner return home than Joseph learns that Herod's son and successor, Archelaus, is an equal threat. Joseph is once again warned, and he goes away with his family to the district of Galilee. How is he warned? In a dream, which he believes.

If I were to ask you, "Do you believe your dreams?" you might say, "I don't dream." Now our friends the neurologists will tell us that we all *do* dream, and a fair amount at that. In the face of that evidence, you could say, "Well, maybe so, but I don't *remember* my dreams." Nonetheless, I would surmise that for many of us, there *are* subconscious ways of knowing that elude empirical explanation, yet that we actually recognize and trust. These ways of knowing have informed how we have made significant decisions in life. There is a kind of "discernable guidance" that taps into the depths of our soul in a quite personal and quite trustworthy way, and this guidance is a significant part of our life history. Dreams, visions, hunches, intuitions, coincidences, impressions, and visitations form a tapestry of meaning for us. This may be difficult and even embarrassing to talk about, but it is also undeniable and very real.

I recently shared a conversation with someone who was facing a significant decision in life. The stakes were quite high, he told me, and he didn't know how he was going to be able to make the decision. How should he be praying? How would he know what to do? he asked me. Well, I told him, *I* didn't know. But I was aware that this person had lived enough years to have had to make major decisions before. I knew that some of these decisions were undeniably good decisions. So I asked, "How did you know before?" When he had made a decision about getting married, about pursuing a particular vocation, about living in a particular place, how did he recognize God's guidance? What did he look for? How did he decide? Did these significant life experiences have anything in common in terms of the tools of discernment that he had used? He responded that it wasn't even *that* conscious. This was not "hard science," he acknowledged. But there *was* a deep knowing, and he knew the landscape and the signs and trusted them. For this person, these tools of discernment were all in the categories of dreams, visions, hunches, intuitions, coincidences, and impressions.

If we were to tabulate in the Bible the amount of the scriptural text given over to the reporting of dreams, visions, prophecies, angelic visitations, and other indirect references to God's mysterious and yet undeniable leading of people, we would find these phenomena comprise approximately one-third of the Bible. These ways of knowing are not insignificant. Yet they are quite countercultural for many of us who live in the Western world. There are some things we unlearn as we grow into adulthood.

Somewhere along the way of your formation into adult-hood, you likely began deferring to reason. You came to claim what you can rationally quantify, compute, defend, explain, and adjudicate as the way—and always the best way at that. This is how we navigate and do our business and science in the Western world. (It's *not* how artists function.) By saying this I'm not negating the use of reason or hard science. That would be silly. I'm simply saying that science by itself is not enough. Life is deeper than that—something we understand innately as children. Children have other ways of knowing that adults are prone to discount as imagination, and yet they are very real to children. In children we witness this God-given capacity to know, to see, to hear, to dream, to realize, to imagine, to play, and to understand on many levels. Many adults have unlearned some deeper ways of knowing, seeing, hearing, and dreaming. The story is told of the eminent psychologist Carl Gustav Jung, who had a conversation with a chief of the Pueblo Indians, Ochwiah Biano. Jung asked the chief's opinion of white people, and was told that it was not a very high one. White people, said Ochwiah Biano, seem always upset so that their faces are covered with worry. He added that white people must be crazy because they think with their heads, and it is well known that only crazy people do that. Jung asked in surprise how the Indian thought. Ochwiah Biano replied that, naturally, he thought with his heart.

There may be a great gift waiting for you by reappropriating God's channels of revelation to you now. First, reflect on how you have known God's revelation in your own past. Stretch back to your childhood if you can. What has helped you get to this point in your life, given the navigations and decisions that you've had to make? Are dreams, visions, hunches, intuitions, coincidences, and impressions part of your own history of knowing? What tools of discernment are planted in the ground of your being, on which you can draw more intentionally? You might find it helpful to put a pad of paper beside your bed for the morning, to help you be more attentive to what of your soul is being mirrored in your night's sleep.

Second, ground new revelation in some other point of revelation you can trust. If you receive a revelation in the form of a dream, ask God for another confirming dream. If the revelation is in a line of poetry or a passage of scripture that emerges out of your memory, does it have a kind of integrity? Is there a sense of continuity in it with who you are or where you are or what you are or where you thought you were headed? Or is this revelation just coming out of left field? If it's "left field," then perhaps it's best to wait. Wait for a bridge to be built in your soul through another word or thought or memory that creates a continuity with where you've been and where you are and where you thought you were headed. (And if that bridge isn't built, let it go.) For some of us, we've learned the importance of sharing our revelation with someone else whom we can trust. Self-deception is such a slippery slope. Not long ago I was sharing a revelation from God with one of my brothers in the monastery, someone who knows me well. He listened carefully, then said to me, "Well, that's certainly convenient. . . ." He reminded me why this "revelation" couldn't be so. Quite. It was rather humbling yet very helpful. So share your sense of revelation with someone who says their prayers, who knows you well, and whom you trust. There's a wonderful phrase in the Book of Proverbs: "Iron sharpens iron and so one person sharpens the wits of another" (27:17). Look for a confirmation of God's revelation.

Third, take heart. If you find yourself praying for God's guidance, God is guiding you already. The desire itself is a seed of revelation. God has caught your attention. In those moments, perhaps your prayer is not, "Where *are* you, God?"

for God is already there in the question or your sense of need. Instead your prayer might be, "What are you trying to show me, gracious God?" You know how it is that you've come to know other things in this life, and this is no mystery to God, who created your inmost parts, is acquainted with all your ways, and from whom nothing is hidden (see Psalm 139).

Fourth, you are not alone. You may already recognize times of confluence between you and God because of something going on within you or around you. It's when a rainbow fills your eyes or harmony fills your ears or laughter fills your heart. You likely know times when you are aware of being prepared or provided for or protected or rescued in ways that you cannot explain, and yet cannot deny. You may know times when you have been visited by a stranger—maybe someone on the street or in a hospital or across a table or at a store or along a path—a stranger whose presence, whose words, or something about them feels congruent and good.[1] We read about such times in the Psalms, "For he shall give his angels charge over you, to keep you in all your ways" (Psalm 91:11). At these moments we are under the ministry of angels beckoning us Godward, inviting us into a dance we share for all eternity. You are not alone.

Last of all, do what you want most deeply. God, who knows you and loves you, created you with a will. You are not a robot. You are not a clone. When it comes to the gift of God's guidance, it's not a package deal. It's a personal gift that comes out of your own history. So get in touch with your deepest desires. Look for them to be confirmed. And then do what you want, to God's glory. When I'm moving in a particular direction, I often ask God to close a door or turn off the light or change something that I would clearly recognize if that way is not the best way, and otherwise I move freely and desirously in this certain direction, to God's glory. Do what you want. To use an angelic metaphor, I might call this "winging it" in God's presence.

Will you always get it right? No, not likely. So desire to be attentive and faithful to the myriad ways of God, Emmanuel, God with you, and you will find God directing you, impressing you, guiding you, alluring you, loving you into that place we see as our eternal home. Follow the bread crumbs!

What is God revealing to you now, in this season of your life? What's your sense?

Day 3

DECEMBER 28

The Gift of Forgiveness

IN MATTHEW'S GOSPEL, Peter asks Jesus, "Lord, if another member of the church sins against me, how often should I forgive?" You can get in touch with the energy of this question by recollecting saying to someone (or maybe *not* saying it but only thinking), "If you ever say that again or do that again, I will. . . ." Will *what*? Whatever that vow is, it is probably not about forgiveness.

Peter here is incensed by the indignity of being offended one time too many by the same person and maybe for the same reason. Peter may have a hunch that some kinds of insults or injuries or lapses are going to continue to happen in life. These come our way not just with our "real" enemies but with most anyone, including those we love. Jesus picks right up on the question and seems to presume the same thing: that various kinds of insults or injuries or lapses are going to happen—and keep happening and keep happening and keep happening—within the life of a community. How many times will these breakdowns likely occur? Jesus says to count on them happening seventy-seven times (Matthew 18:21–22)—code language for saying "endlessly." Peter isn't asking how to deal with inconveniences or disappointments in life, like when a child tips over a glass of milk at the supper table or when someone bumps into you in the elevator. No. That's life. That happens. Peter is asking how to deal with others' lapses, in the face of our own feelings of rage, resentment, and revenge. In those cases Jesus says that we're to forgive and keep forgiving.

These words are stronger still in the context in which they are remembered. This is Matthew's Gospel, about the ordering of community life. It's clear in Matthew's Gospel that Jesus thinks of community in very much the same way that we now think of the world as community. Our CNN-type worldview plus the internet remind us daily how interconnected is our global community. Jesus' words about forgiveness have a currency and poignancy on all levels at which we find membership in community—in our families and friendships, in our vocations and avocations, in our intercultural and international relations.

The absence of forgiveness for the inevitable conflicts that emerge in life in community will obstruct the channel of love. Forgiveness is so key to Jesus' teaching and practice because of his foundational teaching that informs all of our relationships, even with our enemies (see Matthew 5:43–48). Not so many years back, I would have presumed that Jesus' words about "enemies" were intended for other folks, but had little to do with me. If I lived in Haiti, Iraq, the Sudan, in Jerusalem, or on the West Bank, then I would be able to identify my enemies, so I reasoned. But I, personally, have none, thanks be to God. Now I have to admit that this perspective was formed by the Midwestern subculture in which I was raised, which valued the virtue of pleasantness next to godliness. It was not nice to have enemies, and so I did not have enemies. But I've changed my mind on Jesus' notion about enemies and forgiveness. There may not be people who are out to lynch me, bomb me out of house and home, or exterminate my friends and family, but I *am* aware of the almost-daily experience of someone's "crossing" me. I am well experienced with the irritation of someone's interference, of my getting the short end of the stick because of what I think is someone else's selfishness or insensitivity.

Because I've learned to be polite and have been told not to judge others, I would never have dreamed of calling these other souls my enemies. Yet I believe they actually do fall into the category of folks Jesus has in mind. They are persons who don't seem to be helpful to my program, at least for the moment. For the time being, they are irritations or impediments, those whom I may well be tempted to "wipe out," if not literally then at least from my consciousness and care. But if they don't fit into the category of family or friend or neighbor, then they *must* fit into the category of enemy, because those are Jesus' only categories for people: family, friend, neighbor, enemy. And Jesus calls us to love them all. It's a very tall order.

I've changed my mind about enemies in several ways. For one, Jesus tells us to love our enemies, not because it makes for more pleasant living (though undoubtedly it does). Rather, we're told to love our enemies because they may also be our teachers, perhaps even our best teachers. Our enemies can get us in touch with "our stuff" like no one else can. From where do our outbursts or eruptions or emotional responses come when confronted by an enemy?

I am often aware that my own reactions are disproportional to the offense I've experienced from another. Our enemies expose us, and I believe that they are extraordinary agents for our own conversion. When the roughness of someone else's "Velcro" sticks to our own "Velcro," there's something there to attend to *in our own selves*. I'm not saying that the other person doesn't have their own "stuff," too, but that's their stuff. My friends adore me; my enemies expose me. My friends "cover" for me, often overlook my character flaws, are infinitely kind. They are wonderful channels of love. I need them. Yet I also need to reverence my enemies, who are often agents of revelation and often my best teachers. *My* enemies are not necessarily *God's* enemies. I would not want to presume that. *My* enemies are *God's* children, with a place in God's own heart. Jesus calls us to bless them—not to curse them—to love them and forgive them.

In English the verb *forgive* comes from the Latin *perdonare* (from which comes our word *pardon*). *Perdonare*, from *per-* "thoroughly" and *donare* "to give," therefore means to give thoroughly and wholeheartedly. To forgive is to wholeheartedly give it up. It's an offering, an act of "oblation." What would it mean to "give up" a person's offense? I'm not talking about forgetting it. No, quite the contrary. I'm talking about remembering it, and giving it up, like we do with the bread and wine at the altar. We bring to the altar the elements of our lives and labors as an offering, and this includes others' offenses against us. We give up our own selves and others whom we carry in our heart to be transformed, and we do it all in the remembrance of Christ.

The image that Jesus uses for not forgiving someone is "to bind them up" (Matthew 16:18–20). This is to get *even* or get *on* or get *off* by tying them up, chaining them down so they will get what they deserve. To not forgive someone, to "bind them up," is to imprison them. Imprisonment often keeps people from moving and changing. With prisons there's sometimes very little distinction between the prisoner and the prison guard. Both of them are in the prison. Forgiveness is about *un*binding another soul, setting him or her free and thereby setting ourselves free. If we don't forgive, we may end up victimizing ourselves, being in tacit collusion with those who would otherwise make us prisoners. Forgiveness is about setting both them and ourselves free. How often do we do this? Endlessly. This may need to happen an infinite number of times—seventy times seven in biblical shorthand. This may be a way for you to pray without ceasing, of taking the endless offenses, insults, injuries, and lapses that you face, maybe each day, and seeing them not as obstacles but rather as invitations in your relationship with Jesus and the "kingdom on earth" he is intent on building with your help.

For some of us, these words about forgiveness may hit close to home. In English we have this expression about someone "being their own worst enemy." Some days, you may be your own worst enemy. Where forgiveness needs to begin in your life is with yourself. You may not feel you have your act completely together, and in weak moments, you perhaps view your own self with disdain. If that is true, for whatever reason, you likely have lots in yourself to forgive.

Forgiving and being forgiven may be the most difficult thing in life because it is so powerful and so deeply rooted in the memory of our soul. I think that many of us need some help in this area. We particularly need help if offenses have been repeated (seventy times seven), and perhaps even repeated generationally. Often, the help we need is time, time to heal. Painful situations are also sometimes very complicated and very tragic, so we need protection or distance before forgiveness can even be contemplated. But whatever the pain and whatever the offense, I would say that forgiveness is the direction in which to be heading, and that the art of unbinding is to be cultivated, instead of the captivity of binding up.

The wars of the world and the strife in institutions and among family members and friends always begins in individual hearts. Do things within your own power that make for peace. First, make a truce with yourself and with the forgiveness you need. Then look for Christ's invitation to set in motion the power of forgiveness that can unbind a lifetime of despair and hostility. If you are in need of forgiveness, ask for the gift. If you need to forgive, give the gift.

Day 4

DECEMBER 29

The Gift of Joy

NOT LONG AGO I was flying home to Boston from the West Coast. The weather was stormy, the turbulence had been nauseating, and flights had been delayed and canceled left and right. Late in the afternoon the skies were definitely not friendly, nor were my fellow passengers. I had just gotten off one late plane, hustling in a kind of anxious daze to get to my next gate, where I both hoped and feared that my connection would also be late. Then the most amazing thing occurred.

Here in an airport lounge are half a dozen couples, dressed to the hilt, as handsome as models in *Vanity Fair*. They seem to be an official welcoming troupe engaged by the city or a convention. Actually they are dancers, ballroom dancers. Amid the cacophony of airport announcements and all the bustling and bumping that goes on, these six or so couples are waltzing to the music of a string quartet. I stop dead in my tracks—as does most everyone else. People's luggage simply slides down their legs to the floor. They watch, mesmerized, beaming with delight. A man standing near to me—a high-powered executive type—has tears streaming down his cheeks. It is that beautiful: the music, the form and flow, and the gorgeous grace of these dancers. It is such an absolutely arresting juxtaposition to the organized chaos in the airport that afternoon.

It comes to an end, this waltz, only for one of the women dancers to walk through the empty space created by us travelers who had circled around this angelic troupe of dancers. This woman walks to the edge of the circle to a man, simply another traveler, a guy with a plane to catch. He looks as much a mess as the rest of us. He, too, had been absolutely arrested by the dancing. It was more than dancing, it was this choreographed joy-of-the-moment. The woman dancer whispers something to this traveler. Very curious. What is this? He sets his briefcase on the floor and allows himself to be escorted into the center of the improvised dance circle. The music begins again, and within seconds this man, a fellow stranger along the way, starts waltzing with this dancer before us all.

It was a stunning moment, resplendent with energy and flow and delight. It simply soared with the movement of a crescendo. Our fellow traveler seized the opportunity, and it *so* smacked of life. It was pure joy! The spontaneous and thunderous applause we all gave completely drowned out the sorry weather that afternoon.

To have joy or—as we would say in slang—to *do* joy, is to rejoice. To rejoice is to have a deep sense of delight. The Greek word literally means "for the heart, in its deepest place of passion and feelings, to be very well." Joy is something of a rare commodity. The gift of joy does not get much press. Why is that so? And how can this spiritual gift be tapped and unwrapped?

First, joy takes time. Joy is not fast food. It comes as a by-product of living a savored life, of having time and taking time to "smell the flowers." Joy needs time. There is this old monastic insight about living a joy-filled life. Take time, take at least *some* time each day, to do *one* thing at a time. Take time, take at least *some* time each day, if you are walking, to just walk. Take time, take at least *some* time, if you are looking, to just look; if you are listening, to just listen. If you are sipping iced tea or watering the plants or petting the dog, take time to do just that. Do one thing at a time, and do that as often as you can. Take the time to let the fragrances and aromas of life penetrate to the deepest part of your being, where they can be savored. I think we call this "being there." I don't think it has so much to do with the pace of life as it does with the intentionality with which we live our lives. It presumes that each moment is pregnant with God's real presence and provision and promise. Look for it; wait for it; savor it. Don't just visit life; life needs time in order to be lived abundantly.

Second, joy requires acceptance. Joy requires our saying yes to life, to the life we've been given, to the hand we've been dealt, to the invitation to dance. Joy requires a deep willingness to accept how little of our life is actually within our own control. It's an acknowledgment and an acceptance that God will be God: that it is God's world on God's time, that we are God's creatures, and that God is at work according to God's good pleasure.[2] Joy presumes living with intentionality to accept the good gifts of life that actually *are* there, not to live life in a state of rejection or resentment for what is *not* there or *no longer* there. Life brings arrivals and changes and departures, and *that's* life—the changes and chances of life.[3]

To rejoice is to say yes to what is there. Without that quality of acceptance of what is there, those unmet desires of the future can never become present. Without the recognition of what is "now," those unmet desires will always be elusive. In God's good plan, there is a reason why today is not tomorrow. We need the provisions of today to prepare us to receive the promises of tomorrow. Joy requires a posture of acceptance, of saying yes to life: *not* the life we could have had or may feel we should have had, but of saying yes to God for the life that God has given us—which is the only place where there is life for us.

Third, joy requires desire. I was talking with someone not long ago on this topic of joy. There was absolutely no joy in her life, she was saying. I asked her whether she wanted to know joy—well, she had never thought of it quite that way, about wanting to know joy. My question applies to you, too: Do you want to be joyful? Joy is a gift; it's a spiritual gift. Generally speaking, if you want to receive a gift, don't keep your hands in your pockets. Open your heart and open your hands to receive the gift of joy. Cooperate with God.

Last of all, joy requires endurance. Particularly in the New

Testament, a great deal of the writing about joy is in the context of suffering. Why is it that we hear so much about the joy of the cross of Christ?[4] Why is it that at the annunciation Mary first knows fear and then knows joy? It's the same with Joseph: first fear, then joy. And it's the same with the shepherds: first fear, then joy. Much later, it's the same with the women at the tomb: joy comes out of fear, of all things! In the beatitudes, why is it that Jesus says you are set up to be blessed when "people hate you and when they exclude you and revile you and defame you on Jesus' account"? "Rejoice in that day," he says, "and leap for joy" (Luke 6:22–23). How curious. Why is it that Jesus says in John's Gospel, "Very truly I tell you . . . you will have pain . . . but your pain will turn into joy"?[5] How is it that Saint Paul could write from prison to the Philippians, as he was about to be executed, commending us to "rejoice always" (Philippians 4:4–9)?

Joy is a paradox. Our English word *paradox* comes from the Greek *paradoxa*, *para* meaning "other," and *doxa* meaning "glory": "other glory." In other words, it's about God's glory being manifest in a way *other* than we would have imagined. There is a direct relationship between the depth of suffering and the height of joy. The extent to which we have known suffering is the extent to which we can know joy. It doesn't mean that we should go looking for suffering: there's surely enough of it to go around without looking for it. Nor does it mean to deny suffering. It is not a *de jure* principle: first you get suffering and then you get joy, like first you eat your vegetables and then you get dessert. No. It's simply *de facto*. This seems be the way it is. In our suffering in life, when we face what we would not have chosen but cannot avoid, at these times our experience tells us that when we say yes to God, the door is opened for transformation and consecration. The psalmist writes, "Weeping may spend the night, but joy comes in the morning (Psalm 30:6)." There is something about facing the dark night that allows us to see the dawning of joy.

Back in my high school years, I set out to be a competitive swimmer. Several weeks into my first season, I was a broken man. Every muscle in my body hurt. My neck hurt. My shoulders hurt. My arms hurt. My back hurt. My thighs hurt. My calves hurt. I was at my end, and I was sure that I would fail and never make the cut for the team. In my youthful desolation, I poured out my heart to one of the wise old men on the swim team (I think he was eighteen years old). I told him of the absolute despair of my heart and the pain of my body. I remember he listened patiently, and then said, "Do your feet hurt?" "What?!" I asked. He said again, "Do your feet hurt?" "Well," I said, "no, *at least* my feet don't hurt." He said, "They will!" He continued, "You're getting in shape! This is what it takes." Well, I was in ecstasy. Everything still hurt in my body, but my heart soared to the heavens. I was right where I belonged. My suffering was not for naught. This slight, momentary affliction was preparing me for something more and something wonderful.[6] I was suddenly full of ecstatic joy!

Joy *is* a mystery. It's as mysterious as our suffering, and it's as boundless as our suffering. Somehow, in God's economy, the one creates space for the other. Recall Jesus' parting prayer (for you!) in John's Gospel: "Holy Father, protect them . . . that you have given me, so that they may be one, as we are one. . . . Now I am coming to you, and I speak these things in the world so that they may have my joy made complete in themselves."[7]

Go ahead, *do* joy. (Try it, you'll like it!) Joy will not spare you suffering, nor did it spare Jesus. We are not spared the cross; we've shared the cross—but also the joy that follows. Joy *will* give you a place in your heart to be well, to be passionately alive, even amid the changes and chances and sufferings of your life. If you know something already about suffering, then you are at least halfway there. You are "set up" to unwrap the gift of joy in this season of your life. Truly. "May the God of hope fill you with all joy and peace . . ." (Romans 15:13).

Day 5

DECEMBER 30

The Gift of Hope

HOPE IS A WONDERFUL spiritual gift to claim when you cannot foresee the future or when you are traveling an uncharted course in life. Interestingly, the traditional symbol for hope is an anchor. An anchor will hold you fast and keep you from drifting, and yet, pulled up and stowed, an anchor also travels with you as you sail ahead in life. Hope is a "steadfast anchor of the soul," we read in the Letter to the Hebrews (6:19). Hope is something that rests deeper in the water than what happens on the stormy surface of life.

For Saint Paul, all that we do and every step we take is underlined by hope. We live by hope, he reminds us. Most everything else in life is fleeting, and yet "faith, hope, and love abide" (1 Corinthians 13:13). I'm wondering if that rings true for you: does "hope abide" in you during the difficult times and in the opportune times in which we are living?

Hope is an expectant desire that something will come, that something will change, that a way will open: a way *out* or a way *in* or a way *up*. Hope is expectant desire. It is both expectation and desire. Expectation alone is not hope. Desire alone is not hope.

There are things we desire but don't at all expect. They may have to do with a person or place or position or outcome that we want to have or know or experience, maybe desperately. We desire it, but we don't expect it. Is it going to happen? No, not a chance. There are things we desire and don't expect, but that's not hope. That's just wishful thinking or a daydream or a delusion.

Likewise, there are things we expect but don't desire. You may expect that you'll be audited by the IRS or that one of your colleagues will be disappointed or angry with you or that you will have trouble with your allergies. You may expect something but not desire it, but that's not hope. That's a preoccupation, an anxiety, or even a nightmare.

But hope is a melding of expectation *and* desire. Hope is expectant desire. It is a sense of the possible—a sense that something will change, that something will come. Hope is fueled by the presence of God in our lives. But hope is also fueled by the future of God in our lives: a small seed that perhaps we cannot even see right now, planted by God into the ground of our being. We have a sense of it long before we can see it and realize how it will blossom. Hope is adventurous. Hope is open for surprise. Hope lies in what is possible, not what is predictable.

We don't hope for the impossible when we sense it *is* impossible. Nor do we find hope in things that can be easily or automatically obtained. (On a December day in Boston, you would not say, "Today I hope it will be cool outside, not hot." You are already fairly assured of a cold, wintry day, gratis.) The only time we might use the word *hope* for something that *is* gratis is when we have some doubt that we'll actually be able to *have* it gratis. The old Latin term for this is *bonum arduum*, "a steep good." Only a "steep good" is hoped for, that is, something that does not already lie within reach of the outstretched hand, something that *might* still be denied us, though we *do* have a sense, even still, that we will likely have it. And that is hope.

And so we have hope that the price of gas will come down, that someone's plane will arrive on time, that someone we love will be well, that there will be an intervention to the violence in our cities and in our world. These are things we cannot guarantee will happen. But we do have hope for them.

Without hope, we don't act or function. We have no energy because we have no sense of the possible. And when we're at a point of hopelessness, the pain is so intolerable that it may go underground into depression, addictive behavior, or self-deception.

Hope moves us into the future. Hope looks to the next step, whatever it is, whatever form it may take. If there is hope, I take the next step. Hope is not particularly spectacular, nor something we save just for a crisis. Hope is present in each moment as it looks to the next. It is present everywhere in the flowing of the bloodstream and in every small action. We move into the future because of a sense of hope. I would not get out of bed in the morning without a sense of hope. I would not breathe if I did not hope that the air around me would respond to my call. Everything in our physical bodies works for the same reason. We hope that the muscle will work if we move, that the eye will see if we look, and that the ear will hear if we listen. We hope that cars will stop at stop signs, that the food in the supermarket is not spoiled. We also hope that our families and friends and Church will survive, that the governments of the world will work together for justice and peace.

Hope *is* there in your life, if only in a seedling form. How can you nurture these seeds of hope in your soul?

Demarcate what is hopeless in your life. You can protect the seeds of hope in your life by marking off the areas of hopelessness and acknowledging them in order to face them directly, not with despair but with the intent of keeping them from infecting all the areas of possibility in your life. Undoubtedly there are skills you do not have, situations that can be overwhelming, challenges that are intimidating in your life. These are "hopeless" areas of your life where you probably need the gift of courage or companionship or humility. It can make a remarkable difference in your life to keep sorted what is hopeful from what is hopeless. Areas of hopelessness are a factor in all our lives. So name them, claim them, demarcate them, get help with them. Meanwhile, don't miss claiming the wellsprings of hope in your life.

Nourish the gift of hope from your own memory. What can you learn from looking backward in your life that will help cultivate the seeds of hope for the unknown future? There's a charming passage in the writings of Lewis Carroll in *Alice Through the Looking Glass*. Speaking to Alice, the

Queen says, "And that's the effect of living backwards. . . . It makes one a little giddy at first . . . but there's a great advantage in [your] memory working both ways." Alice, rather dubious, responds with caution. "I'm sure [my memory] only works *one* way. I can't remember things before they happen." The queen retorts, "It's a poor sort of memory that only works backwards."

Draw from your miracle memory what you already know about sailing in uncharted waters. How in the world have you faced what you've had to face to get to where you are? You are a walking miracle. You are also an experienced navigator. Recall Saint Paul's formula, that we "boast in our sufferings, knowing that suffering produces endurance, and endurance produces character, and character produces hope, and hope does not disappoint us, because God's love has been poured into our hearts through the Holy Spirit that has been given to us" (Romans 5:1–5). Hope is an anchor amid the storms of life.

Last of all, notice a subtle but important distinction between hopes and hope. They are like cousins, but they're not exactly the same. Hopes are glimpses of things we wish for and see or can imagine, and they grow out of hope. Hope is anchored in things we cannot see. Saint Paul writes, "For in hope we are saved. Now hope that is seen is not hope. For who hopes for what is seen? But if we hope for what we do not see, we wait for it with patience" (Romans 8:24–25). If you want to find the difference between hopes and hope in your life, I suggest you try something quite drastic. Make a list of three different things about which (or in whom) you have hopes for change. They can be related to your self, your family, your work, your future. Three things you can see or imagine—these are hopes.

Now draw a line through these things. They're not going to happen. (Of course, I could not know for sure what will happen with your list, but go along with me here and suppose that none of this will come to be.) See if you can pry yourself from these three things on your list. Are *you* still there? What is left, after you've seen your hopes come and go, is hope. Whatever sense there is that we can go on, that we will make it, that there is somehow sense and purpose and a future—though your hopes be dashed—is hope. What's left is, I think, what Saint Paul calls "abiding hope."

For a number of years, Joan Erikson worshiped with us in our monastery chapel. Joan was an acclaimed playwright, poet, dancer, and artist, married to the great developmental psychologist at Harvard, Erik Erikson, her best friend and collaborator. At the time of Erik's death, Joan wrote a short love poem that was read at Erik's funeral. The poem is titled "Hope."

> The word "hope" the learned say
> Is derived from the shorter one "Hop"
> and leads one onto "Leap."
> Plato, in his turn, says that the leaping
> of young creatures is the essence of play—
> So be it!
> To hope, then, means to take a playful leap
>   into the future—
> to dare to spring from firm ground—
> to play trustingly—invest energy, laughter;
> And one good leap encourages another—
> On then with the dance.[8]

If you have a memory to look back on your life, and if you are unable to see clearly into the future, remember that nonetheless the seedlings of hope are undeniably present. Cultivate the gift of hope.

Day 6

DECEMBER 31

The Gift of Redemption

A MAN CAME TO SEE ME not so long ago to talk about his beliefs as a Christian. Actually he spoke mostly about what he could no longer believe. He named a whole list of "stuff" that he couldn't "buy" any longer. I think he presumed I would challenge him or make him feel guilty. Instead, I just listened to his list and eventually said, "Why don't you forget it all? Forget all this religion stuff. That was then; this is now. Why don't you give yourself wholeheartedly to something like rose gardening or gourmet cooking or hang gliding? It sounds like you need to get a life."

Well, he was shocked. Monks are not supposed to say such things. No, of course he could not walk away from his religious faith, he told me. So what was going on inside of him, he asked?

I said he probably did believe something about God, or he would not have known his doubts. I told him that the something was probably God, or was of God. Probably. And I would say that to you, too. If your former experience of "God" no longer has enough meaning for you, if it's too small, too pedestrian, too local, too convenient, then translate it. Find some new language to speak out of the depths of your soul, lest you confuse your experience of God, or your thoughts about God, as God. God is always more. God comes to us from the future. God is always more. If God is not something more—more, in ways beyond which you have thought or imagined or experienced—then God will likely be something less, probably something created in your own image.

What don't you believe any longer? Have you been spiritually weaned from something you once held dear? I'm not in any way suggesting that in the past your belief in God or your experience of God was not real or true. Nor am I suggesting that God was not really present in the ways you once knew or sensed God, the ways in which you came to depend on God, see God, love God, and serve God. Quite the contrary: in Christ Jesus, we see how God is prepared to meet us on our own plane. In Christ Jesus, God comes to us to catch our attention and bid us follow in ways that are familiar and safe and inviting, and then to lure us on, like with bread crumbs, to food that will last forever. God is always more, in ways beyond those we could have thought or imagined or experienced. If God were not ever greater, then we would risk reverencing the archives of our experience of God rather than worshiping the living God. God is always more, and creates in us a life-longing for more. I suspect that for many of us, God will leave us with less so that we have space and desire for more. We often experience God's alluring presence far more in our own experience of God's real absence. God comes to us in our hungering for, thirsting for, desiring after, and longing for God, to use the language of the Psalms.

Believe less. I'm not suggesting you willy-nilly discard a verse from the Bible here, a phrase from the Nicene Creed there, a historic Christian doctrine that you don't fancy. I'm not suggesting tossing but rather reclaiming. You may find yourself just now rather scattered or confused, feeling you've lost your spiritual anchorage because of things that are going on. Go deeper; go to the bedrock of your soul where you're not confused. In Jesus' own day, there were endless rules, doctrines, principles, practices, and commandments.

It seems they were not altogether helpful to everyone's program. So when Jesus was asked, "Teacher, which commandment in the law is the greatest?" Jesus answered: "Love God with all your heart, and soul, and mind." That's number one. And number two: "Love your neighbor as yourself" (Matthew 22:36–40). If you find that in this season of your life you cannot believe more, then believe less, something profoundly less—but profoundly essential.

To believe is not ultimately to wrap your brain around some existential concept. To believe is to embrace something with your heart, as if your life depended upon it. The English word *believe* comes from the same etymological root as the word *belove*, which is to hold dear, to love deeply.[9] Believe; belove. Go deeper. Get out of the confusions of your head and go deeper into your heart. Conform your life around the priority and practice of loving God with all your heart, soul, and mind, and of loving your neighbor as yourself.

Where to start? Start with what is most immediate: yourself. Inside your soul, you may be yelling at yourself right now. Perhaps a part of you is yelling that you should be better or different, and the other part is saying forget it, this is the way it is; you're doing the best you can. There may be a part of you that's not on speaking terms with your whole self.

If there's something unforgiven or seemingly unforgivable in your past, you need to get over this. You may need some help. For you are not going to be able to love your neighbor any better than you love yourself. And I think that the love of God—your love of God and God's love of you—will become very present and very real as you sort out these other two loves: for yourself and for your neighbor.

Or perhaps your life is in pieces. There's been this, and there's been that. Some of it has been good; some of it, not. Lots of things have gotten broken and lost. *You've* been broken and lost. Let me tell you: the strands of your life do weave together into the most amazing tapestry. It does all hold together. Some of us, if left alone, only see the inside, the back side of the tapestry, where there are lots of stray threads and knots and pulls. The front side is often quite a different picture. The way the shape, form, color, and design hold together is how others, who know us the best and love us the most, see us. And this is also how God knows and sees us. Most of us, if left alone, are quite myopic and can't get a true perspective on the amazing grace of our life. We need to be saved from that mean shortsightedness about ourselves, to pray for "the eyes of our heart to be enlightened" to see ourselves as God sees us.[10] If there are pieces in your past that you think don't fit in your present, I would probably beg to differ with you. It all belongs somewhere, somehow. God is very frugal in this way. Claim all you are that has brought you to this extraordinary moment in life. When Jesus says he's come "to seek and to save the lost," he is speaking to you (Luke 19:10). Wherever you are in touch with loss, Jesus has come to retrieve and restore and redeem it. It all belongs. Claim it.

In the vocabulary of the Church, we call this redemption. Nothing is wasted; nothing is to be wasted. It all belongs. It all forms part of this majestic tapestry called "your life," like no other. Claim the gift of your most amazing life.

Day 7

JANUARY I

The Gift of a Name

ACK IN MY EARLY elementary school years, one of my biggest fears was that someone would discover my middle name. Nobody but my family knew it. And it was also all their fault. My middle name is Gustaf, a Swedish name passed down from my paternal grandfather and my own father. I had feared that I would end up being nicknamed Gus, the archetypal "dumb Swede." The prospect of being called a derogatory name *because of* my middle name was a considerable source of childhood anxiety, and so this was one of my greatest childhood secrets. That is, until one day around about age nine, I discovered that I shared my middle name with the king of Sweden: Gustaf![11] That revelation was immediately transforming. I suddenly thought: maybe I am of royal blood? I probably am! I simultaneously went from being deeply embarrassed about my middle name to becoming almost unbearable because of it. I made sure that everyone knew my middle name. It was as if my discovery gave me a new identity—because there is power in a name.

Oftentimes great care is taken in the naming of a newborn child. The child's given names may be a sign of the continuation of a family's heritage, or the given names may be a sign of a family wanting to start anew, signified in the birth of this child. The child's name may express identity or hope or gratitude. Through the name, the parents may seek to bestow dignity or particular significance on the child's birth. Sometimes names demarcate a family's own timeline. One of my nephews has a Saudi Arabian middle name because he was born while his father was working in the Persian Gulf. As children grow up, they often will take on new, imaginary names, and with the names, new exploratory identities. One summer, as a young camper far away from home, I told my new cabin buddies that they should call me Butch because I was tough. It worked pretty well for a week at camp, but my new sought-after identity evaporated when I returned home and had to face my eye-rolling sister and my baby brother. He certainly didn't know me as Butch.

He was still struggling to simply say "Curtis" or "Curt," which he could not pronounce. Most of the time he called me "Durt"—"Hi, Durt!"—which hardly suited someone of royal lineage.

As children grow up, they will name their belongings, and they shall possess everything they name. Many children will suffer the wound of being called a name. Maybe it's to be taunted with their given name, twisted into something cruel or comical sounding. Maybe it's a name that jeers at some physical trait the child bears. Maybe the name mocks the child's ethnic or religious heritage. Maybe the name is a sign of others' jealousy. On the other hand, the child might be given an endearing nickname, perhaps a diminutive, as a token of affection. I recently received an e-mail from an older acquaintance named Edgar, who is a wise and much-respected person of great stature. His e-mail address is "edgarito" (little Edgar), which is how he was affectionately known as a child. Very endearing.

In the political world, great intention and ceremony is given to naming parks and benches and fountains, buildings and bypasses, highways and tollbooths, economic programs and military campaigns. Universities name their endowed academic chairs. Fundraisers name their benefactors in annual reports and on wall plaques. Books are dedicated in the name of those dear to the author. In the advertising world, the greatest imagination and care is taken in naming new products like perfumes, medications, detergents, cars, roses, or toys. The name needs to both fit the product and also form its image. In life everything important has a name. In naming there is the power of identity and identification, whether it is the name of a person or a place or a creature or thing.

It is equally true in the Bible. There seems to be a pre-occupation with names and naming. In the creation account in the Book of Genesis, Adam is given a name. Legend goes that he named most everything else in sight—everything from animals to children—because in naming, things and people are set apart. Our name is what uniquely distinguishes us *from* others; however, our name also unites us *to* others insofar as others will call us by name and therefore can know us and have a certain claim on us.

In our scriptures, especially in the Psalms, there is a frequent reverencing of the name of God. In Psalm 8 we hear, "O LORD our Governor, how exalted is your name in all the world!" In Psalm 31 we hear, "For the sake of your name, lead me and guide me." Psalm 145 begins: "I will exalt you, O God my King, and bless your name for ever and ever." It's a curious phrase. to bless God's name or to praise God's name or to petition God, for the sake of God's name. How dare we have such intimate access to God as to lay claim on God's name? So great and awesome was this God, whose ways were unknowable, whose power unpredictable, whose transcendence unfathomable, whose rage uncontrollable, whose face unseeable, whose hands untouchable, whose name unknowable and unspeakable.

And yet, this God, Creator of all, who is otherwise beyond our grasp, takes on face and form in a child of Bethlehem. This very God is re-presented in our world, born just like we are, with hands and a heart and eyes, with desires and expectations and fears, and given a name: Jesus. The name both identifies Jesus—that is, sets him apart from us—yet also gives us access to him.

Do you know the experience of a friend's telling you, "When you have your meeting, when you talk with so-and-so, go ahead and use my name"? In the world of business or diplomacy, we call this a referral. In the political world, we can call this a lobbying effort. In the world of friendship, we can call this a welcomed connection. In the world of our prayer, we call this an intercession or supplication. Some days I think our best prayer to the God whom Jesus named "Father," our best plea or best praise, is simply to "name-drop," to use the name that God has finally shared with us: Jesus.

How do you occupy your in-between time? When you are waiting for an appointment, on hold on the telephone, in your car at a red light, on a runway awaiting take-off, what do you do? What do you do in the wee hours of the night when you are sleepless yet again? Where is your attention while you walk from this place to the next, wait for the water to boil, the mail to arrive, the news to come, the baby to be born? Those moments can be vacuous, and you may find yourself prone to obsess over all kinds of distractions or anxieties. Especially during these moments of space, you might find it inviting to breathe the name of Jesus. Breathe in the name of Jesus; breathe out the name of Jesus. You might even find it inviting to pray the ancient "Jesus Prayer" as you breathe:

Lord Jesus Christ,
Son of the Living God:
Have mercy upon me.[12]

Knowing someone's name gives a certain access, intimacy, and power. You have Jesus' name. Use it. Breathe the name of Jesus as you make your way through the day. Breathe the name of Jesus for yourself and for others, those far off and those who are near. Jesus will live up to his name for you. Breathe the name, use the name "Jesus," because there is power and identification in claiming and using and sharing a name. Go ahead and use it, the gift of knowing the name Jesus: Jesus . . . Jesus . . . Jesus. . . .

Day 8

The Gift of Humility

As a young man, I was very earnest, and set out to practice the cultivation of various spiritual gifts, among them, humility. I worked at it with fervor. In a short time, a number of my closest friends intervened, saying that my working so hard at being humble was helpful neither to them nor to me. I had become insufferable, predictable, overly pious, and not much fun to have around, they said. My attempt to become humble was to them an experience of my rather naïve pride. "Give it a rest," they pleaded. For humility is a gift, not a skill to master. Humility is like a secret that everyone else knows about you, but from which you are kept in the dark.

Humility comes as a by-product of living a well-practiced life. The English word *humility* derives from the Latin *humilis*, "lowly," "near the ground," *humus* being the earth, "gravity," as Saint Paul says. For those of us who are followers of Jesus Christ, his lowly birth in Bethlehem should ground any sense of pretense we can have as Christians. The prophecies that anticipated the coming Messiah consistently speak of the Messiah's humility: "Lo, your king comes to you, triumphant and victorious is he, humble and riding on a donkey" (Zechariah 9:9). Jesus himself takes up this theme of humility when he speaks of how we should enter his coming kingdom: Enter as a little child.[13] Those who exalt themselves, he says, shall be humbled, and those who humble themselves shall be exalted (Luke 18:9–14). His point is that we should not think too highly of ourselves— our opinions, our pedigree, our education, our positions, our good looks, our charm or eloquence. Elsewhere Jesus says, "Take my yoke upon you and learn from me; for I am gentle and humble in heart, and you will find rest for your souls" (Matthew 11:28–30).

A spiritual practice that will clear the space in your soul for humility to take root is hesitating. By hesitating, I am not talking about being demure nor about being spineless. I'm speaking here of reverencing those whom you find alien. Many of us, if truth be told, will find certain people to be uninteresting or ignorant or insufferable. This may arise from their appearance, habits, beliefs, age, education, ethnic origins, dress, tattoos, or piercings. You may find yourself being dismissive, disgusted, or damning. You are prone to be judgmental of these souls.

Our exercising judgment is necessary most every day. All of us are trained to be quite judgmental people; our "critical faculties" are an essential part of life. Some of this is simply pragmatic, like our judging whether it's safe to cross the street, or judging the weather to determine whether we should wear a jacket or carry an umbrella. At a deeper level, many of us regularly find ourselves having to judge people: whether we can trust them; whether we can support their desires or plans or aspirations or requests; whether we will say yes to speaking with someone, to being seen with someone, to lending our name or word of support to their cause, to sitting at table with them, to socializing with them, to voting for them. We have to make judgment calls about confrontations and interventions. We must judge when someone has done too little or gone too far, overstepped a boundary or raised an issue too many times. We must exercise this kind of judgment on the job or among our family members and friends, where we must judge a stance or tack

GIFT OF HESITATION

we will take. Sometimes by making judgments, we run the risk of being misunderstood and therefore having to pay our dues twice.

GRACE / WISDOM

In judging other people, however, if we only go so far as damning or distancing ourselves from these various other souls, if we only go so far as separating ourselves from them, then our judgment has probably not gone deep enough. Our critical faculties, used unavoidably and essentially in life, are a domain within our soul that invites an ongoing conversion to Christ. The real invitation for our own judgment of others is for us to faithfully reflect the nature of God's own judgment. This judgment is the grace of being able to see not through someone but into someone. It is the grace to see the conditions that make them happy and fulfilled, that give them a sense of belonging, that plague them with suffering and doubt, that cripple or consume them. Here judgment is the grace to see into someone as God would see into someone—no matter who they are, friend or enemy—as someone for whom God has an eternal love. This judgment is the grace of being able to see life at a deep level, and this is wisdom.

What would the spirit of humility actually look like? For starters, it would mean taking a posture of hesitation, not presuming that you've got it right in the face of someone whose story and beliefs, values and practices may be very different from your own. In God's eyes these others are surely not outcasts; they are God's children, and they may well be our teachers. A spirit of humility is nurtured by a posture of hesitation, seeking to listen to, learn from, and reverence the other. It seems to me that North American Christians have an awful lot to learn from the world around us, which God so loves. Jesus says to us that "the last shall be first" (Matthew 19:30, 20:16; Mark 10:31, 13:30). The last place you might have imagined yourself looking for God's presence, the last person to whom you would be inclined to give any heed or hearing or deference or care, may be the first place to look, especially if God's presence to you seems unclear in these uncertain times.

Jesus preaches one gospel and opens his arms very wide, for all. In Christ there is the movement away from separation *from* others, to compassion *for* others, to identification *with* others. The founder of the Society of Saint John the Evangelist, Richard Meux Benson, spoke not just of living *for* another person but living *in* another person. This person whom you may be quick to discount or disown or reject: you are this person. This person is closer to you than a brother or

63

sister. I would call this the "grace of identification," the healing of our poor judgment to see ourselves in the face and form of the other.

If you find yourself being quick to judge, prone to being rather hot-tempered, consistently surrounded by people who are inadequate or clueless or slow or boring or irreverent or just plain poor examples of what you think a person should be, you may be at least halfway there in learning about the grace of hesitation. We can learn well from those circumstances in which we are *not* prone to be hesitant at all. Your proclivity to be quick and condemning may be like a Pavlovian bell ringing in your soul. Pray for the grace of awareness when you find yourself being judgmental in a damning way. Ask yourself: What has this occasion awakened in me that requires me to be superior or dismissive or condemning or grateful that I am not like this other person? I think we can most learn the grace of hesitation, of waiting on or waiting for another, by using the experiences of life where we are most *un*hesitant. Pray for the grace of awareness, which will often proffer the grace of hesitation—because there's always more going on than immediately meets the eye.

Some of us may judge ourselves, and do so quite harshly,

especially when we come up short in terms of productivity or dependability or accountability. Those are the days when our own character flaws can get the best of us and the best of others. That is when our life's preparation seems inadequate for the tasks at hand, when the burdens we bear are intolerable and unacceptable and yet also unavoidable. When it comes to judging ourselves at the end of the day, we may consistently score a poor mark. And we likely judge others the way we judge ourselves. The fruit of humility is the conversion of our critical faculties from a rejecting meanness to a generous mercy, the judgment of love and the grace of identification with others. We belong to one another: one God, one world, ultimately one table at the great "messianic banquet" to come. We see in Jesus the nature of God's judgment, which is a judgment of love.

The gift of humility is sown into our soul at birth and consummated in our death, both of which are lowly experiences where we are not in control. In the meantime we can cultivate this gift, not by focusing on ourselves but rather on others, in the dignity we bestow on them by reverencing them—their lives, values, traditions, opinions. Make space for others in your own heart as God makes space for you. Practice hesitation, a posture of holy listening to others' lives.

You will be the last to know about this gift, but it will be something that others recognize as the gift of humility.

A final word of comfort. The words to the familiar Christmas hymn "O Little Town of Bethlehem" were penned in the late 1800s by the great Boston preacher and bishop Phillips Brooks. It may be a familiar hymn, but it is hardly an innocent hymn, either for Phillips Brooks or for us. He wrote this hymn following a visit to the Holy Land and in the aftermath of our own Civil War. In the course of ten years of war in our own land, more had died and by our own hands than in the entire previous history of the nation. To Phillips Brooks and to many of his contemporaries, there was enormous fear and no assurance that there would be a future. Could we as a nation re-collect ourselves and rediscover God in our midst? The nation was terribly frightened and desperately humbled. In this great hymn, the phrase, "Where meek souls will receive him, still the dear Christ enters in," may be to you a word of comfort. If you find yourself these days feeling uncharacteristically meek, already rather humbled by the circumstances that surround your life or fill your heart, you are in a perfect position to meet this Christ child, eye to eye. He comes to us, lowly, for the lowly. Receive him anew.

JANUARY 3

The Gift of Companionship

O N SATURDAYS AT OUR monastery, it is our practice to especially remember the Blessed Virgin Mary, mother of our Lord Jesus Christ. Do you already value her companionship? You may come from a religious background where the remembrance of Mary was very much a part of your spiritual formation. Or you may hold the remembrance of Mary with some suspicion, thinking that she may get in the way of your relationship with Jesus. To you Mary may simply be a porcelain fixture in a Christmas crèche, with no other meaning one way or the other. Welcoming Mary to travel the way with you may be a great gift.

For some down through the centuries, Mary, mother of our Lord, has made God accessible. It is all, otherwise, far too male. If the God whom Jesus called Father is too hidden from you just now, too ferocious, too exacting, too awesome, you might find some comfort in access to Mary, who seems to have God's ear, as someone to whom you can safely whisper your desires or despairs, trusting that that message, through her, will get to where it belongs. Hers is a kind of nascent safety, a kind of nurturing and knowing that many mothers embody. It may be true of your own mother. It may be true about the mother you never had—because, perhaps, she was snatched from your own life far too early, or because she was far too scarred by harsh experience, in which case both you *and* your mother may need a mother. Tender, tenacious Mary's presence may then make the house of God approachable and safe. She incarnates the *anima* in us all: the one who receives and conceives, who carries and holds, who bears tears of gladness and grief, who miraculously knows when the fullness of time has come.

You might find a kind of kinship in Mary because of your own sense of inadequacy and unworthiness. Here we remember Mary, probably a teenager, likely illiterate, with an inauspicious pedigree, certainly unwed, being told she will bear something too great. It will be wonderful—and it will bruise her life. If Mary's first reaction to the angel's announcement was fear, surely others' (perhaps most others') reaction to Mary's pregnancy would have been disbelief or disdain: a kind of sneering incredulity, perhaps not unlike your own reaction today, were some teenage girl to report to you that she was pregnant, not by a boy but by a Spirit. Such a story! I think it's more likely that Mary's story was written off, that the "real" story murmured behind closed doors was that she had conceived out of wedlock, that this son of hers was neither the Messiah nor was he even "legitimate," as they say, and probably did. And though the record of the Gospels remembers her as being faithful, I suspect that many others in her own lifetime remembered her as being a fraud, and they consequently rejected both her story and her son's. You may know deep in your heart what it is to be misunderstood and to be maligned. Mary, for you, may then form an intimate bridge of connection between your beginning and your end. Before you can grasp your need for salvation, you need to make peace with your creation, and Mary comes to you as a holy reconciler.

You may be in touch right now with fear. It might be fear of the unknown. It may be fear of the known, some seed of a sense you carry in your heart—or in the pit of your stomach—of what you sense God is calling you to be or to bear or to birth. Mary's first response to the visitation of the angel—telling her what she was to bear—was fear. Mary may then be a companion to you in your fear.

You might find a keen identification with Mary because of Mary's costly calling. It's the burden of being blessed. You, too, know what it is to be visited by God, calling you to survive, calling you to be or become or bear something in this life that only few could understand and that many—perhaps even some who are close to you—might *mis*understand. In this case, you may find yourself keenly identifying with Mary's first response of fear: how can it be, what you are to bear and become, given the inadequacy of where and what you've been? You may keenly identify with Mary's existential mystery, an amazing loneliness, given the uncharted unfolding of your own life. You may very much understand Mary's response to God's angelic visitation—how can it be?—given your own childhood or adolescence, given the unfolding of your story in your prime of life, perhaps in the last chapters of your life. "How can it be?" And then finding yourself, like Mary, saying to God, nevertheless, "Be it unto me, according to your will . . ." (Luke 1:38).

You may know the experience of resisting or resenting something that has been unfolding in your life, perhaps something that is costing you too much, seeming to threaten your very existence—and then you wake up some morning and realize that it's going to be okay, and you find yourself being able to say yes to life again. I think this is some of Mary's experience when she was called by God's angel to be the Christ bearer. Her first reaction was fear; her second reaction was puzzlement—"How can this be?" And then she awakens to what is being asked of her as something she can, in fact, do. She says to God, "Okay. Be it unto me according to your word." You may know what it is to finally say okay to God, to make peace with your destiny. Perhaps then Mary may be to you an ally as you face your own impossibilities to find the freedom to say yes to what is clearly and unavoidably being asked of you in life just now, to say, like Mary, "use me, take me, call me as you will."

You might look to Mary's prayers on your behalf especially at times when your own prayer is parched or overwhelmed or full of sighs too deep for words. We call this kind of prayer "intercession"—someone speaking on behalf of another. I would say that the space is very thin that separates us from those who have lived before us and who have passed from this life into the next. I might not need to convince you here that there is some kind of enchanting, graceful connection we may find with our forebearers, maybe even that their care for us in this world has been converted into prayer for us in the world to come. I might not need to convince you that there is some kind of connection, a communion of saints and communion of souls, between this world and whatever comes after—and that it is good, very good. Mary then may "be there" for you in the celestial throng, someone whom you understand and whom you understand understands you. In her is a form of heavenly advocacy for you with her Son or with her Son's Father, in ways that you know or want or need.

And finally, you may find in Mary some deep inspiration as a companion to someone's suffering. You may know someone well, love them deeply, carry them in your heart, laugh when they laugh and weep when they weep, and yet, in the moment of their deepest suffering, find yourself mysteriously repelled, knowing the temptation to leave them, abandon them, create some distance from them—not because you don't love them but because their suffering is so great, and you don't know if you can abide it. Here we have Mary, this image of the *pietá*, holding Jesus in his suffering, finding the strength and courage to stay with this loved one who suffers. She may become a courageous companion to you and your loved one in the hour of suffering.

Ask for the gift of Mary's companionship:

Hail Mary, full of grace, the Lord is with you.
Blessed arc you among women, and blessed is the
      fruit of your womb, Jesus.
Holy Mary, Mother of God: Pray for us sinners
      now and at the hour of our death.

Day 10

The Gift of Gratitude

EING THANKFUL IS the most powerful gift in life. Gratitude transforms our own lives and makes us really present to the extraordinary gift of life. Your own practice of gratitude will make you real and will permeate the life around you like fragrance from a flower. Start small; start now. If you find yourself, at this very moment, being able to sit upright in a chair without having to be strapped in, be thankful. If you are able to rise to your feet without another's help, be thankful. If you can hold a cup of coffee, if you can drink from that cup using the coordination of your own muscles, be thankful. If you are now breathing without mechanical assistance, be thankful. When you awaken in the morning, if you can hear the alarm, be thankful that you can hear. If you have a water tap in your home, a bed on which to sleep, a light overhead, be thankful. If, when you look outside your window, whether you see the sunshine or the rain, for the very fact that you can see, be thankful.

Being thankful is much more than a polite duty. Being thankful actually addresses a deep need we all have: a need to be recognized and acknowledged and remembered for the gift of who we are and the gift of what we do. I imagine some of the same needs in God, in whose image we have been created. God must get something out of being thanked and praised, at least as much as we do. There is delight in being thanked. It turns a duty into a gift.

I first learned this in a theater, not while on stage but while in the audience. I remember the first play I saw as a young boy. I was fascinated by the playbill, how everything was so carefully scripted—except, it turned out, for one thing that happened at the very end. As the final curtain fell and the stage lights dimmed, the audience sprang to its feet—unprompted. The event was simply made complete by our thunderous applause and great cheers. The actors undoubtedly needed to hear our gratitude, but what brought us to our feet was *our* need to express gratitude. There is something about expressing gratitude for something or for someone that completes the experience.

If prayer—your relationship with God—in any way eludes you just now, simply pray your gratitude. Gratitude in prayer is like oil to a frozen gear box. Gratitude is like a liquid fertilizer being added to the plant water. Gratitude is a spiritual angioplasty. Don't miss the opportunity to pray and savor your gratitude for what is so clearly good in life. Be grateful for the gift of life. This is a way for you to "pray without ceasing." Don't miss any opportunity to express gratitude to others. It will transform their day and perhaps their life.

Living life gratefully, with contentment, is a spiritual practice that can easily escape us. Be content. The English word *contentment* comes from the Latin *contentus*, which means to be "satisfied" or "contained." There is an old monastic principle about living life to its fullest and freest. Freedom is known in the context of limitations. This is quite countercultural. Western culture identifies us as "consumers," part of a market economy that is constantly alluring us with *dis*satisfaction, where what is next or what is new is presumed to be better than what is now. There's the sense that more *is* more and never enough. We hear, "Keep your options open," and "Keep your commitments few." The notion that what is, is enough may be quite radical. And yet I think there is buried treasure to be found in the grace of contentment, of living thankfully in the present moment.

Contentment is not passivity. To be content is not to be seduced into thinking that to be complete we must stretch our soul ever broader, ever thinner, to take in ever-new experiences, to buy new toys, taste new pleasures, hear new things, master new skills. Rather, contentment is to grow our soul downward, deeper, into the ground of our being. Contentment is an active living into the depths of what it means to be living life now, today, given all the givens. Contentment is more about being than it is about doing or acquiring or mastering or disciplining or craving or searching. Contentment is a needed complement to redress all the doing that our life and vocation require. Contentment is about being satisfied given the limitations of our present life. The psalmist says, "Out of the depths, O Lord, have I cried to you; Lord, hear my prayer" (130:1). And in another place, "Be still, and know that I am God" (46:10). I would say that it is in stillness, in letting be, in being enough, in saying yes to the life we've been given now that the grace of contentment is to be discovered and savored.

Contentment is a necessary complement to the "movements" of life. We know that Jesus was often on the move. He says more than once to his followers, "Come, follow me." He sends his followers out: "Go into all the world," he says. He talks about laboring and sowing and harvesting. But he also talks about being. Simply being can be elusive and an art that is often lost. "Abide with me," we hear Jesus saying in the Gospel according to John (see chapter 15). "Stay with me," he says. What we're after is this sense that the incompleteness of life as we experience it now is enough. What we need is already here. The treasure for which we search is likely buried under our own feet. Jesus says, "Do not worry about tomorrow, for tomorrow will bring worries of its own. Today's trouble (and, I would add, today's provision) is sufficient for today" (Matthew 6:34). Live into what is already at hand. Jesus commends that we learn the secrets from the flowers of the field. "Consider the lilies," he says. "Look at the birds of the air" (Matthew 6:25–33). Likewise, the great Christian mystic of the fourteenth century, Julian of Norwich, found the truth of all being by meditating on the mystery and majesty of a hazelnut.[14] Saint Francis of Assisi found Christ's invitation for gratitude in the profound simplicity of the created order that surrounds us:

Be praised, my Lord,
for all your creatures,
and first for brother sun,
who makes the day bright and luminous.

Be praised, my Lord,
for our sister, mother earth, who nourishes us and
watches over us
and brings forth various fruits
with colored flowers and herbs.[15]

There's an old French proverb: "Gratitude is the heart's memory." There's an extraordinary grace in looking backward on your life. You will see things from a new perspective. What may have seemed a senseless loss, some unmitigated pain or tragedy, likely shaped you into the person you are today. Even in the most difficult passages of your life, you will likely find a wellspring of gratitude. The same event, which you thought would be a "killer," if looked back on now will oftentimes seem like a miracle. Even underneath the kinds of losses we experience in life—people, relationships, opportunities moving on or changing or dying—underneath the kind of deep grief or anger we may feel for that wonderful thing, that beautiful person or relationship that is no more: beneath that dark feeling is thankfulness, because it has made all the difference in the world to who you are. You would not be who you are without that experience in your past. Oftentimes, underneath the kind of anguish we experience with the changes and chances of life, there is gratitude. If we will only dare to go down deep enough into the well of loss, we will find there is actually a ground spring of thankfulness just waiting to be drawn out and recovered and expressed. Mourning is often disguised thankfulness waiting to be expressed. It can make a world of difference to look backward in your life.

Living our lives in a posture of gratitude is an acknowledgment that we are not the author of life but a participant in life, and that it is God's world on God's time, and that God is at work in our lives according to God's good pleasure and on God's time. God has all the time in the world. God is obviously not in a rush. If you are living without all the answers you think you need, give thanks. Give thanks to God that God knows what you do not know. In God's eyes we are always children, regardless of our age, and children are not developmentally ready to know everything at once.

There's a reason why today is not tomorrow. Don't cut in line in life. Live the incompleteness of your life with gratitude. A century ago, Rainer Maria Rilke wrote:

> I would like to beg you to have patience with everything unresolved in your heart and try to live the questions themselves as if they were locked rooms of books written in a very foreign language. Don't search for the answers, which could not be given to you now, because you would not be able to live them. And the point is, to live everything. Live the questions now. Perhaps then, someday far in the future, you will gradually, without even noticing it, live your way into the answer.[16]

If you are out of practice expressing thanks to God, the conduit of gratitude between you and God may be plugged up. You may not realize how much God desires not only to be thanked by you but to be thankful for you. God longs to thank you for what you are to God and what you are of God to God's children and God's creation. Teresa of Ávila, the sixteenth-century Spanish nun and mystic, said that "Christ has no body now on earth but yours, no hands but yours, no feet but yours. Yours are the eyes through which Christ's compassion is to look out to the world. Yours are the feet with which Christ is to go about doing good. Yours are the hands with which to bless all people now." God is enormously thankful for you. You make God's day; you represent God's presence here on earth. God does not take you for granted, and is eternally grateful.

Pray and practice living your life with gratitude in every way you can. It will not make your life come round rosy in every way, nor will you evade the difficult challenges that life brings. But living life gratefully will rebalance your life, enlarging what is so clearly good to new proportions. Gratitude will make you really present to life. Living gratefully will inform your whole life with meaning, from childhood to eternity.

The Gift of Peace

ECEIVE THE GIFT OF PEACE. The world of first-century Palestine gave peace coming and going. *Peace* was commonly used as a word of greeting and farewell (see, for example, John 20:19,21,26). *Peace. Shalom. Salaam.* This is a gracious salutation, an expression of desire. "Peace to you!" There was as much hope for peace in Jesus' day as in our own. People would have been "all ears" to hear Isaiah's prophecy that the coming Messiah was named the Prince of Peace (Isaiah 9:6–7). In the Gospel record, the conversation about peace soon moves from the innocence of the crèche to the violence of the cross. A grown-up Jesus speaks of peace in an atmosphere of hatred and rejection, where there was every prospect that his own followers would meet a death similar to his own. Jesus says, "Peace I leave with you;

my peace I give to you; I do not give to you [peace] as the world gives" (John 14:27).

"Peace as the world gives" is dependent upon outward circumstances. It was then and it is now. When we read in the newspaper that there is a call for peace in Jerusalem or Baghdad or Kabul, this will be marked by the absence of conflict. In Jesus' day, the notion of peace for the neighboring Greek culture was essentially the absence of strife or war. But for the Jews, peace had little to do with outward conflict. "Let not your hearts be troubled, and do not let them be afraid," Jesus says. There's going to be trouble, but don't be troubled. Jesus says, "I am leaving you. And yet, I am leaving you with a gift: peace." The peace will be mediated by what Jesus calls "the Spirit." Jesus breathes the Spirit on them, not unlike a mother ever-so-gently blowing on the face of her child who rests in her lap. That's the tenderness I imagine in Jesus breathing this Spirit of peace upon his disciples.

Jesus is speaking neither a gracious salutation nor an expression of desire, nor is he speaking in the absence of conflict. He is offering us a gift of peace. We could actually call Jesus' gift an offer. A gift only becomes a gift when the recipient receives it. I could say to you, I have something for you: this book. I present it to you. I offer it to you. But it only becomes a gift when you take it, when you receive it. Gifts require reception to become gifts, otherwise they're simply offers. This offer and promise of Christ's peace is here for the having. Receive it. Take it in as regularly and necessarily as you breathe. This requires attentiveness because there is so much that can distract us or hold us hostage by worry and fear. Here are some suggestions to help you keep in good practice receiving the gift of peace:

- There may be some word that becomes a breath prayer, a mantra that helps keep you aware of your need for peace and Christ's provision of peace.

Breathe out fear;	Breathe out anger;	Breathe out sadness;
Breathe in peace.	Breathe in peace.	Breathe in peace.
Breathe out fear;	Breathe out anger;	Breathe out sadness;
Breathe in peace.	Breathe in peace.	Breathe in peace.
Breathe out fear;	Breathe out anger;	Breathe out sadness;
Breathe in peace.	Breathe in peace.	Breathe in peace.

⧫ You may know a phrase from the Psalms that you breathe softly, repetitively, as an elixir to spiraling down into despair:

◊ The Lord is my shepherd; I shall not be in want. (23:1)

◊ Show me your ways, O Lord, and teach me your paths. (25:3)

◊ As the deer longs for the waterbrooks, so longs my soul for you, O God. (42:1)

◊ For God alone my soul in silence waits; from him comes my salvation. (62:1)

◊ Bless the Lord, O my soul, and all that is within me, bless his holy Name.(103:1)

You may practice the gift of peace with some movement of your body, some posture that you assume in your private prayer or that you incorporate as you walk and work, something with your body—maybe a bowing, the lowering of your head, some gesturing or signing with your hands.

⧫ You may practice the gift of peace drawing on your senses:

◊ Using an icon or other image on which to gaze in
  your home or at your work.

◊ Using touch, whether to finger prayer beads or
  a hand cross or a spiritual medallion; perhaps to
  enjoy or give a therapeutic massage.

◊ Using the gift of smell from a beautiful flower or
  some inviting aroma that fills your lungs and soul.

◊ Using the gift of hearing, listening to music that
  evokes the memory of Christ's gift of peace and
  invites harmony into the depths of your being.

◊ Participating in some program of serenity that
  helps you stay aware and open to the ultimate
  power and provision of Christ's peace.

I'm not talking here about making peace. There is plenty
of peace that needs to be made all around our world and on
our streets. That is undeniable. This peace here, which Christ
offers us, antedates our being peacemakers. This is about our
being peace-receivers, practicing a posture of reception of
peace. If there is war somewhere in your own heart, if you
have places where you are not reconciled with your own
past and are bound up by unforgiveness, if you're assaulted

by envy or jealousy or hate or revenge or rage, then you need a truce in your own heart . . . because we do love our neighbors as we love ourselves. Peace in our own hearts will change the world.

Receive the peace of Jesus.
Receive the peace of Jesus.
Receive the peace of Jesus.

Day 12

JANUARY 6

The Gift of Blessing

THE GIFT OF BLESSING from God is the assurance of well-being. It is a promise of provision, our sense of being "the apple of God's eye," of having a place in God's heart. In the scriptures, this sense of blessing is pervasive. In the Old Testament, the word often used for blessing is *barak*, which has a curious history and etymology. The origins of *blessing* go back to the primitive religions of the Middle East. Blessing was connected with the fertility of crops, animals, and human beings—and thus provision for the future. A sign of blessing is the evidence of more: more substance or more goodness. Prosperity, in every form, becomes the sign of God's blessing in the Old Testament. But in the New Testament, in the light and life of Jesus, this changes. *Now* it is adversity that becomes the touchstone for blessing.

Surely this has something to do with the cross of Christ. In not many days from now in the Christian year, the holy innocence of Jesus in the crèche will have met betrayal, then crucifixion on the cross. Those of us who are followers of Jesus cannot get out from under the cross, the paradox for Christians. Jesus promises to give us abundant life. The way in which he speaks about it is by way of the inevitability of the cross. We are shared, not spared, the cross. We hear the grown-up Jesus saying, "If any want to become my followers, let them deny themselves and take up their cross daily and follow me. For those who want to save their life will lose it, and those who lose their life for my sake will save it" (Luke 9:23–24). Our theology hangs on the cross. And we either pick it up or stumble over it, because it most certainly is there for those of us who choose to follow Jesus.

Jesus promises God's favor, God's care, God's provision, that God's love can be known in the best of times and in the worst of times—which you can probably best understand if you've been there. Jesus says, "Blessed are you who are poor, for yours is the kingdom of God. Blessed are you who are hungry now, for you will be filled. Blessed are you who weep now, for you will laugh. . . ." If you have been to the brink of life, if you have cried out to God like Jesus did from the cross, "Why, O why have you forsaken me?" and then miraculously lived to tell the story, you probably know something about the mystery of blessing that can come through the greatest of adversities. What was undeniably and perhaps unexplainably bad has in some miraculous way been redeemed as a channel of God's light and life and love. And *that* is the paradox of God's blessing, where you can neither deny the bad—when you've been weeping or hungry or in some other way tormented—nor deny the blessed good that somehow the one has prepared the way for the other. The French theologian Leon Bloy says, "There are places in the heart that do not yet exist, and then suffering enters so that they might exist."

There is another curious quality about this promise and provision of blessing. *We* are given power to bless, and we mirror that blessing back to God and all that God has created. In this way, life is like an icon: we look on God through the same eye that God looks on us. God who is blessed is the God who blesses. We hear in the Psalms, "May God be gracious to us and bless us and make his face to shine upon us" (67:1). And in response, we pray with the psalmist, "Bless the LORD, O my soul, and all that is within me, bless his holy name" (103:1). "Bless the LORD, O my soul; O LORD my

God, how excellent is your greatness! You are clothed with majesty and splendor" (104:1).[17] The theologian Martin Israel writes of the mystical tradition, saying that there is nothing in this world that is unholy; there is only that which has not yet been blessed. This is not merely a Christian insight, but an earlier Jewish insight that Jesus himself inherited and transformed.[18]

In blessing God, we are telling God that we take none of it for granted: our life, our labor, our loves are all gifts of God. Blessing is letting *God* know that *we* know that God is the beginning of life and the end of life and the way into all life. I'm not really sure what God "gets out of it," if you'll pardon my slang. But it seems that God enjoys being praised at least as much as we do. There is an ancient belief that God is in some way empowered or energized by our blessing, by our praise and thanksgiving. Maybe you can understand this quite personally. Do you know, from your own experience, how your being praised and thanked and your feeling empowered all seem to go hand in hand? Just as we are "empowered" by being praised and thanked—by being blessed—it must also be so for God, because we have been created in the image of God. Our praise and thanks to God—our blessing God—makes a difference to God.

The psalmist writes, "Every day I will bless you, and praise your name forever and ever," which must thrill God no end (145:2).

We stand before a table and bless the food, be it bread and wine or a roasted turkey at a holiday table. We bless people on their wedding day. We bless water at baptisms. On Ash Wednesday we bless ashes as we begin the season of Lent. We bless icons. We bless crèches and crosses, houses and fountains. We bless healing oil and a rancher's soil. We bless sneezes; we bless creatures. If you got carried away, you could (rightly) come to think that the whole of life was to be blessed. We bless *God*, and we pray God's blessing on everything else in sight.

Can you receive these words: that you are a blessing to God, and that God is intent on your being a channel of blessing, the blessing of God's light and life and love to all that surrounds you? If you stumble over those words, if you find yourself responding with argument or qualification— "How can *I* be a blessing?"—because your life is a bit tattered or because you are so undisciplined or because there are some shadows in your own life, let me remind you that God is bigger than all that. God has created you as a gift to God's own self, and God is intent on your being a channel of God's blessing. It's of your essence. This is what you've been created to be: to be a blessing *to* God and a blessing *of* God.

Over the course of many years, I've had occasion to visit a small pond in southern Massachusetts. The pond is fed by a freshwater spring, except when some well-intending beavers take up residence, and then the inflow stops. At other times the outflow of the pond is blocked, presumably by relatives of these well-intending beavers. I've seen this pond crystal clear, and I've seen it bracken. If the mouth of the spring is blocked, the pond goes bracken. That may be obvious. But even if the mouth of the spring is wide open, if the outflow of the pond is blocked, the pond will become bracken because it simply cannot receive more fresh water.

This scene from the pond comes to mind in regard to our being a channel of God's blessing. If your sense of God's blessing you eludes you just now, it may not have to do with the source of blessing or the actual presence of blessing in your life, even now. It may have to do with the outflow in your life. If it's in any way clogged or restricted, let it flow. Open it up. Don't be tentative or reluctant or apologetic about your being created to channel God's blessing. You are intended to be a blessing to God and to all that God has created. It's of your essence. Be generous with the light that teems from your eyes; be generous with your words and actions in this flow of God's blessing to God and to others. That outflow may open up your own experience of the inflow of God's blessing you. Let it all flow amid the happiest and sorriest of conditions you witness. Receive the gift of God's blessing, day by day, and share it with great generosity.

1. Hebrews 13:2: "Do not neglect to show hospitality to strangers, for by doing that some have entertained angels without knowing it."

2. Saint Paul writes: "Therefore, my beloved, just as you have always obeyed me, not only in my presence, but much more now in my absence, work out your own salvation with fear and trembling; for it is God who is at work in you, enabling you both to will and to work for his good pleasure" (Philippians 2:12–13).

3. A beautiful collect from Compline reads: "Be present, O merciful God, and protect us through the hours of this night, so that we who are wearied by the changes and chances of this life may rest in your eternal changelessness; through Jesus Christ our Lord" (Book of Common Prayer, p. 133).

4. See, e.g., John 16:19–23; Romans 12:9–13; 2 Corinthians 8:1–2, 13:9; Philippians 1:18–21; Hebrews 12:1–2; James 1:2–4; 1 Peter 1:3–9, 4:12–14.

5. We hear Jesus say: "Very truly, I tell you, you will weep and mourn, but the world will rejoice; you will have pain, but your pain will turn into joy. When a woman is in labor, she has pain, because her hour has come. But when her child is born, she no longer remembers the anguish because of the joy of having brought a human being into the world. So you have pain now; but I will see you again, and your hearts will rejoice, and no one will take your joy from you" (John 16:20–22).

6. Saint Paul writes, "So we do not lose heart. Even though our outer nature is wasting away, our inner nature is being renewed day by day. For this slight momentary affliction is preparing us for an eternal weight of glory beyond all measure, because we look not at what can be seen but at what cannot be seen; for what can be seen is temporary, but what cannot be seen is eternal" (2 Corinthians 4:16–18).

7. Jesus' "High Priestly Prayer": John 17:13.

8. To my knowledge the poem is unpublished and otherwise unrecorded.

9. The word *believe* comes from the Old English *belyfan*, from the "Proto-Germanic" (the hypothetical prehistoric ancestor of all Germanic languages, including English) *galaubjan*, "to hold dear, to love."

10. The phrase "the eyes of your heart be enlightened" is taken from Ephesians 1:17–19

11. I IM King Carl XVI Gustaf.

12. The Jesus Prayer, noted in *The Way of the Pilgrim*, dating from the 1850s in Irkutsk, Russia: "The continuous interior Prayer of Jesus is a constant uninterrupted calling upon the divine Name of Jesus with the lips, in the spirit, in the heart; while forming a mental picture of his constant presence, and imploring his grace, during every occupation, at all times, in all places, even during sleep. The appeal is couched in these terms: 'Lord Jesus Christ, have mercy on me.'"

13. See Mark 10:15f. See also Mark 12:38f, Luke 1:48, Luke 14:11.

14. Julian of Norwich (c. 1342– after 1413) was an English mystic.

15. Francis of Assisi (1181–1226), excerpted from his "Canticle to the Sun."

16. Rainer Maria Rilke (1875–1926). *Letters to a Young Poet: Letter Four* (July 16, 1903). Stephen Mitchell, translator.

17. Psalm 104:1. See also, e.g., Psalms 5:12; 16: 7; 28:9; 34:1; 63:4; 67:1; 84:5,6; 100:4; 103:1, 21, 22; 134:3; 145:1,2.

18. From Martin Israel's writings in *Summons to Life.*